# SUSSEX TRAN
# HERITAGE

Colin Tyson

AMBERLEY

*Front cover:* Volks Electric Railway, Brighton, and Lillywhite's garage on Manor Road, East Preston.

*Back cover:* Hastings West Hill cliff lift.

*All photographs by the author, unless stated.*

First published 2018

Amberley Publishing
The Hill, Stroud
Gloucestershire, GL5 4EP

www.amberleybooks.com

Copyright © Colin Tyson, 2018

The right of Colin Tyson to be identified as the Author
of this work has been asserted in accordance with the
Copyrights, Designs and Patents Act 1988.

British Library Cataloguing in Publication Data.
A catalogue record for this book is available from the British Library.

ISBN 978 1 4456 8061 3 (print)
ISBN 978 1 4456 8062 0 (ebook)

Typesetting and Origination by Amberley Publishing.
Printed in Great Britain.

# Contents

# Introduction

Sussex has always relied on strategic transport links, given its proximity to both London and to its channel ports, particularly over the past 250 years, in order to meet the social and economic changes of its growing population. Sussex roads only improved with the arrival of the Turnpike Trusts in the eighteenth century in response to increased carriage traffic, with their demise coming in the nineteenth century on the arrival of the railways. The railway line from London to Brighton transformed the coastal settlement into a major resort destination and Hastings, Bexhill, Eastbourne, Worthing, Littlehampton and Bognor all followed. Some commuter towns, such as Haywards Heath, owe their existence to being on the main line railway from London, and at their zenith branch lines spread their tentacles all over the county, reaching places that had only previously known horse traffic.

Street tramways in places such as Brighton and Hastings provided cheap urban transport, flourishing briefly in the early twentieth century, only to disappear in the 1930s to make way for the new trolleybuses.

Waterborne transport has left its mark in the county in the form of short-lived canals with their locks and bridges, along with its sea ports and docks.

The purpose of this book is to show a selection of landmarks that all serve to illustrate what can still be seen today as reminders of our glorious transport heritage. Discover the only canal tunnel in the county and its only aqueduct, the toll houses from the days of the turnpikes, railway structures of interest and the 1930s art deco passenger terminal buildings to serve the pioneer passenger aviation industry. If the locations are not immediately obvious, then grid references have been added to aid the explorer.

Sussex is home to Britain's oldest electric railway, the first municipally owned bus operator in the world, the steepest surviving seaside cliff lift in Britain, the destination of the world's oldest motoring event and the first ex-British Railways standard gauge steam railway to be operated by volunteers – which provided the inspiration for over 100 more closed lines around Britain to be re-opened by enthusiasts.

As with all evolving industries, the older, obsolete facilities are in danger of disappearing or are already lost. Railway branch lines have been lifted and have disappeared, although, thanks to local authority initiatives, many can now be explored as 'green lane' footpaths and cycle paths. Even the once-common utilitarian railway signal box is in danger of disappearing under railway modernisation schemes, unless they are listed structures. Happily, a good selection has been saved from destruction.

# Chapter 1

# Roads

The roads and trackways of Sussex that would be familiar to our ancestors were pretty much impassable, muddy affairs, especially during winter and spells of heavy rain – save for the tracks along the chalk ridge line of the South Downs that would have been well-known to pedlars and pilgrims. Much of these tracks now form part of the 100-mile-long South Downs Way National Trail from Eastbourne to Winchester, and when walked today you can still find yourself in splendid isolation, away from the busy commuter towns of the Weald and the coastal resorts.

The A29, looking south towards Billingshurst, formerly the Stane Street Roman road that ran from London to Chichester.

The Romans set out Stane Street – the road from London (Londinium) to Chichester (Noviomagus Reginorum, or 'new market of the proud people') – after their invasion in AD 43 on much of what is now the route of the A29 and can be easily traced as a former Roman road on a map on the stretches both north and south of Billingshurst.

Much of the route of the A27 through Sussex started life as the Roman road from Dover to Exeter and the Romans would also have made roadways to their ironmaking sites in the Wealden forests, only to abandon them before the Wealden iron industry surfaced again in the late sixteenth and early seventieth centuries.

Local iron cinders were used in layers to metal a section of the London to Lewes Roman road that was excavated at Holtye, near East Grinstead, in 1939 (TQ 462389). The fenced and preserved 30-metre length, dated to around AD 100, is 'maintained' by the Sussex Archaelogical Society.

While it fell to local parish initiatives to maintain roads in the centuries that followed, real improvements only came about with the establishment of the Turnpike Trusts, authorised under individual Acts of Parliament. Over fifty individual concerns were active in Sussex from the mid-1700s to the mid-1800s. Early turnpikes included the Surrey & Sussex, which entered the county at Felbridge, through East Grinstead to Forest Row and Witch Cross (now Wych Cross), as well as the road from Crawley to Reigate, with one of the last sections (St Leonards–Sedlescombe and Hollington–Hastings) being established in 1836.

Thus a tariff, or toll, could be charged to passing coaches and animal drovers to maintain the upkeep of principal roads. Many toll collectors combined their duties with other forms of employment, such as agricultural labouring.

The area behind the fencing is a section of Roman road excavated in 1939 at Holtye, near East Grinstead, and is 'maintained' by the Sussex Archaeological Society.

*Left*: The enterprising Mr G. Leney ran four coaches in the morning and six in the afternoon from Lewes to Brighton.

*Below*: The short stretch of the M23 motorway that lies within Sussex, constructed between 1972 and 1975.

Travellers were also assisted by the construction of bridges where necessary and the introduction of the coaching inn, where travellers and their horses could take overnight rest and refreshment. Travel was still slow, however; for example, the coach journey from London to the coast at Littlehampton took some twelve and a half hours in 1778, but by the 1830s had been reduced to a mere ten hours.

Although the improvement to roads under the local authorities during the twentieth and twenty-first centuries need not concern us, it is worth noting that the county's only nod to the motorway age, the M23, extends from Hooley (Surrey) to Pease Pottage to join the A23, the short stretch south from Gatwick being within Sussex.

# Bridges

Built from medieval times to the 1800s, Sussex retains a fine selection of road bridges, from examples at Greatham and Stopham in the west of the county, to Bodiam and Newenden in the east, using stone, brick and, later, wrought iron.

The turnpike era brought Sussex its most early form of a road 'flyover' – a term perhaps more associated with modern roads. At Cripps Corner (TQ 776212) a sandstone and brick arch was erected in the 1840s to carry the Ewhurst to Gill's Green road (Hawkhurst Trust) over the existing Brede Turnpike, and it still does the same job today, carrying the B2089 over the B2244.

The Grade II listed Greatham Bridge crosses the River Arun south of Pulborough and is of fourteenth-century origin. With eight smaller stone arches and two larger, the nearer wrought iron girders were added in 1869 (TQ 032163).

Stopham Bridge also spans the River Arun on the site of a former ford and is now a Scheduled Ancient Monument, being of medieval origin. Major work was undertaken in 1822 when the centre arch was raised to provide extra clearance for vessels using the Arun Navigation and Wey & Arun Canal. The parapets of the replacement bridge can be seen behind (TQ 029183).

Stopham Bridge carried the traffic of the A283 over the river until a new bridge to the north was completed in 1986.

Exceat Bridge carries the A259 over the River Cuckmere. Built in 1876 of wrought iron plate, it consists of a single carriageway, although there are plans to remodel it for today's traffic (TV 514993).

This three-arched stone bridge at Bodiam spans the River Rother and was built in 1796 to replace an earlier structure (TQ 783253).

*Above*: Newenden Bridge carries the A28 road over the River Rother, marking the boundary of Kent and East Sussex. The three-arch stone bridge was built in 1706 (TQ 835270).

*Left*: The oldest-surviving road 'flyover' in Sussex is at Cripps Corner, carrying the Hawkhurst Trust's road over the existing Brede Turnpike, and it is still doing the job it was built for (TQ 776212).

# Coaching Inns

When the section of road between Lowfield Heath and Brighton was turnpiked, the full length of the London–Brighton road was now properly maintained and the journey by horse and carriage only took eight hours. The George Hotel in Crawley's High Street became a coaching inn and was ideally situated as a stopping stage, being at the halfway point between London and Brighton. The building is an amalgamation of many disparate older parts and the original gallows over the road outside is now just a replica. Its exterior is not original, although a section of roofing tiles of local Horsham stone could be.

*Above*: The Chequers at Maresfield is an imposing three-storey Georgian coaching inn. The A22 road now bypasses the village.

*Right*: The George Hotel at Crawley was ideally situated for coach and horse refreshment, being situated halfway between London and Brighton.

The Sheffield Arms, on the A275 at Sheffield Park, is now a retail outlet.

The Georgian period brought several substantial coaching inns, with the best examples being on the A22 at Nutley (formerly the Shelley Arms and now private) and Maresfield (The Chequers), as well as on the A275 at Sheffield Park (the Sheffield Arms – now a retail outlet).

# Milestones

The provision of distance markers, each a mile apart, had to be provided by the Turnpike Trusts under the Acts of Parliament from which they operated. By far the most visible and still maintained by East Sussex County Council are the string of 'bow bells' milestones along the A22 from Lingfield (Surrey) to Hailsham, which consist of iron plates on wooden posts, with features painted black on a white background (early photos show them not painted at all). The posts on the section from Uckfield to Hailsham also depict, above the mileage figure, the Pelham Buckle – the buckle being the badge of the Pelham family, who were important local landowners.

Milestones within towns were a local authority responsibility and there is an example of such a stone in the front wall of the Fifteenth Century Bookshop, situated in the narrow section of the high street in Lewes. It is believed that the stone is younger and of eighteenth-century origin, and that the stone may have been re-set here from another location. It gives '50 miles from The Standard in Cornhill, 49 to Westminster Bridge and 8 miles to Brighthelmstone' (Brighton).

*Above*: A 'Bow Bells' milestone on the A22 at Nutley, 38 miles from London.

*Below left*: A 'Bow Bells' milestone at Maresfield, 41 miles from London, along with a typical example of an East Sussex fingerpost.

*Below right*: A 'Bow Bells' milestone at East Hoathly, now with the addition of the Pelham Buckle over the mileage figure – a feature of the Uckfield to Hailsham section.

*Above*: The milestone situated in the front wall of the Fifteenth Century Bookshop on the high street in Lewes – 'Fifty miles from The Standard in Cornhill'.

*Left*: A typical West Sussex fingerpost of iron with wooden fingers, surmounted by a 'polo mint' location roundel.

# Toll Houses

Toll houses from the days of the turnpikes survive in some number throughout the county. By their nature they were very small affairs – perhaps a former cottage or just a two-roomed bungalow – and in virtually all cases have since been extended in size either along the roadside or at the rear, and sometimes both. The giveaway of course is that in most cases they are still positioned nearer the highway than the later properties around them. Inevitably, over the passage of time, and because they do not enjoy a protected status, some have now been modernised to such an extent that they no longer give any indication as to their former use.

*Above*: The brick and tile-hung bungalow toll house at Amberstone (Broyle Park to Battle Trust), decorated with false timber framing, with two windows facing the road, between which was a central door (now blocked). It is situated on the south side of the A271 (TQ 599113).

*Right*: The Ashcombe toll house (Brighthelmstone to Lewes Trust), situated on the south side of the A27 at the turning to Kingston. Circular, with a cement dome, it was once one of a pair each side of the road at the former entrance to Ashcombe House, erected *c.* 1810 (TQ 389093).

*Left*: Toll table, Ashcombe.

*Below*: Battle, North Trade, toll house (Broyle Park to Battle Trust), a brick bungalow situated on the south side of the A271 (TQ 738160).

Beeding toll house was built *c.* 1810 on a new road from Horsham to Shoreham, established in 1807, and was operated until the Trust was wound up in 1885. It was dismantled in 1968 and re-erected at the Weald & Downland Museum at Singleton in 1970 (SU 874128). The toll board, affixed to the side, came from the Petworth Trust's Northchapel toll house.

East Hoathly toll house (Uckfield & Langney Bridge Trust) is of a T-plan design with a slate roof and was later attached to a Victorian house. It is situated in the village centre on the north side of the former A22 (TQ 523163).

*Above*: Houghton toll house (Storrington & Balls Hut Trust), situated on the north side of the B2139 at Houghton Bridge, near Amberley station, is a flint bungalow with a slate roof that has been extended from its original form (TQ 023118).

*Left*: Lindfield toll house (New Chapel & Brighthelmstone Trust) is unusual in that it is an example of an earlier property being taken over by a turnpike trust. When the gate was removed in October 1884, it was burnt on-site by joyful villagers (TQ 347254).

The grandest toll house in Sussex must be that at Long Furlong (Worthing Branch Trust) of 1802, constructed of brick and flint, with a castellated front. Tolls were collected from the centre window. It is situated on the east side of the A280 (TQ 101075).

Malling toll house (Malling & Witch Cross Trust), a brick (now stuccoed) bungalow with a centre projection to the road. It is situated on the west side of the A26, north of Lewes (TQ 426122).

# Toll Bridges

Several bridges within Sussex were subject to tolls in the past. A swing bridge across the River Arun at Littlehampton was opened in 1908 and tolls were collected from those who used it. The last tolls were collected in 1953, when the bridge was taken over by West Sussex County Council, and a new fixed bridge was completed in 1973. The old swing bridge was eventually demolished in 1980 and its former toll house was moved to Amberley Museum & Heritage Centre and re-erected.

The Old Shoreham Bridge, crossing the River Adur at Shoreham-by-Sea, replaced an earlier ferry and remained in private trustee ownership for its first eighty years. In 1861 it was taken over by the LB&SCR on the opening of the line from Shoreham to Horsham. British Rail finally closed the bridge to road traffic in 1970, which at the time was the last public road bridge in Sussex to be controlled by toll. The bridge is now purely for pedestrians and the road bridge was replaced by a new A27 flyover to the north of the old bridge the same year.

The Norfolk Bridge at Shoreham-by-Sea, also spanning the Adur, was opened in 1833 and was replaced by the present structure in 1922. It was freed from toll in 1936 and the toll house at the Shoreham end remains as a residential property.

The former Littlehampton Bridge toll house now resides in retirement at Amberley Museum & Heritage Centre.

*Right*: Old Shoreham Bridge 6d toll tickets, issued by the Southern Railway and British Railways.

*Below*: Norfolk Bridge toll house, Shoreham, on the eastern side of the now replaced bridge spanning the River Adur. There were once two smaller collecting booths in similar architectural style at the western end (TQ 213051).

# Motoring

Early motor cars were required to be preceded by a man on foot with a red flag, but the need for this was abolished in 1896 with the new Light Locomotives on the Highway Act, authorised by Parliament, raising the speed limit from 4 mph to 14 mph. Harry Lawson, who formed the first motoring club in the UK, celebrated by driving 60 miles from London to Brighton. After earlier local runs, the first Motor Car Club's run to Brighton began in 1899 and only stopped in the war years with petrol rationing. The world's oldest motoring event is commemorated on the first Sunday of each November and provides a spectacle as the vintage cars travel through Sussex down to Brighton.

Some cars were steam driven, some had internal combustion, and there were even early examples of electric cars, but cars were still the domain of the wealthy until the rise of mass private car ownership in the 1960s. Some types of commercial vehicles used steam power until the 1930s, but the petrol engine vehicle was increasing in popularity. An exception was the councils and contractors that still used steam road rollers to repair roads, some right into the 1960s, although motor-driven rollers had been available since the late 1920s. Early commercial vehicles can be viewed by the public at the annual London to Brighton Historic Commercial Vehicle Run, which takes place annually on the first Sunday after the early May bank holiday.

The rise in popular motoring saw an increase in the number of petrol filling stations and repair garages, the two services often being combined.

Participants in the annual London to Brighton Veteran Car Run battle with the modern traffic.

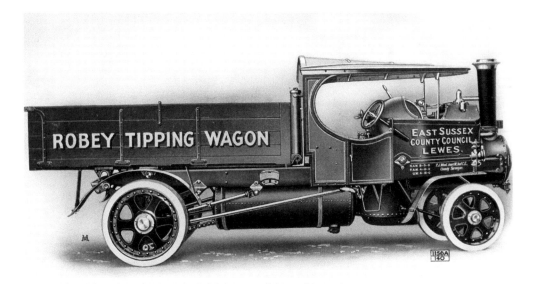

*Above*: Robey of Lincoln 5-ton tipper No. 38506 was supplied to East Sussex County Council on 14 November 1919.

*Right*: Works photograph of Garretts of Leiston steam wagon No. 35369, ready for dispatch to Frank F. Green of Bexhill for hauling road and building materials.

Road haulage contractor F. Avann of Eastbourne purchased Garrett steam wagon No. 35352, which was finished to a high standard.

*Above left*: Foden C Type steam wagon No. 11340 of 1923 was new to Rock Brewery, Brighton, as a delivery dray. A bus body was fitted during the preservation era to replicate the Foden works brass band vehicle. (Malcolm Ranieri)

*Above right*: A sign from the Roads Act 1920.

*Below*: WSCC warning to steam engine operators.

Lillywhite's garage on Manor Road, East Preston, now houses apartments, but has been preserved in its 1930s art deco style.

A typical village service station of a style that was once commonplace.

A disused former petrol pump operator's booth at Rodmell.

A former West Sussex County Council-owned Marshall steam roller undergoing restoration at
Amberley Museum.

*Above*: A typical living van that would be towed by the council's roller driver each week, travelling from one work site to another while away from home. It was new to Midhurst District Council in 1925.

*Right*: Membership of the Automobile Association (AA) and the Royal Automobile Club (RAC) increased with private car ownership. AA members were issued with a key that could open the boxes, which held a telephone and a list of AA appointed garages. Box No. 44 was located at Bucks Green, near Horsham, and is preserved at Amberley Museum.

The best events to see preserved steam road vehicles in Sussex are the Tinkers Park Traction Engine Rally, held in early June at Hadlow Down, and the Wiston Steam Rally, held in early July at Wiston House near Steyning.

# Trams and Trolleybuses

To meet the needs of their growing population, the seaside towns of Brighton and Hastings introduced street tramways, which were later superseded by trolleybus operations. Brighton Corporation Tramways opened on 25 November 1901 to a gauge of 3 feet 6 inches and reached its fullest extent of route mileage in 1938. Six of its eight routes operated from the main base at Aquarium (Old Steine) and the last tram returned to its depot in Lewes Road in the early hours of 1 September 1939 – just two days before the outbreak of war. Just the one Brighton passenger tram survived scrapping for the war effort, F Class No. 53, which is undergoing restoration by the Tram 53 Society. The former overhead line works car now lives a life of retirement as a summer house in a garden at Patcham.

Many Brighton tram shelters outlived the trams, with some still doing the job they were built for as passenger shelters at bus stops, but most have been resited elsewhere. The former tram depot in Lewes Road still functions as a bus depot for Brighton & Hove buses.

Brighton's trolleybus system opened on 1 May 1939, gradually replacing the trams. Unusually, it had two operators – Brighton Corporation Transport (fifty-two vehicles) and the Brighton, Hove & District Omnibus Co. Ltd (eleven vehicles) – although the Corporation owned the wires. The whole system closed on 30 June 1961. Two former Brighton trolleybuses are preserved, but are not based in Sussex.

Brighton tram No. 53, undergoing restoration.

The skeletal interior of Brighton tram No. 53.

Brighton's tram shelters were of oak frames and had doors, seats, electric lighting and pagoda roofs. There were two generations of shelters, basically to the same design but with variations. They were painted brown and cream (as were the trams), and were painted green after 1939. This shelter was on Ditchling Road and is now at Stanmer Park.

This shelter at Amberley Museum came from Dyke Road.

A relocated shelter at a bus stop on Ditchling Road.

This shelter on the railway at Amberley was sited at Richmond Place, opposite St Peter's Church.

Brighton Corporation Tramways Depot on Lewes Road.

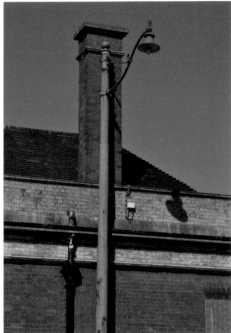

*Above left*: Etched glass window, Lewes Road Depot.

*Above right*: A surviving trolley pole – Lewes Road Depot.

Brighton tram No. 41 on its last service before the system closed on 1 September 1939. (John Bishop Collection)

Hastings & District Electric Tramways began operating in two sections on 31 July 1905, operating independently until 1907. Of 3 foot 6 inch gauge, one system operated in the town centre, with a depot at Silverhill, and the other operated through St Leonards and Bexhill, and finally to Cooden Beach in 1906. A year later the two systems were connected along the seafront. The system closed in May 1929 and was replaced with trolleybuses. Two tramcars survive, Nos 48 and 56.

The new 1928 fleet of trolleybuses included eight open-toppers, making the fleet unique in the world and by 1929 had 21 miles of trolleybus route, then the longest in the world.

*Above*: Lewes Road Tram Depot is still used today.

*Right*: A section of Hastings tramway track from Silverhill.

The preserved Hastings trolleybus *Happy Harold* gives rides at special events.

The system, by now operated by Maidstone & District, closed on 31 May 1959, and four vehicles are preserved, one at the East Anglia Transport Museum, Carlton Colville, Suffolk, and one at the Trolleybus Museum at Sandtoft, Lincolnshire. Two are with the Hastings Trolleybus Restoration Group. One was fitted with a Commer TS3 diesel engine in 1959 and, being self-propelling without the need for electricity, still makes public appearances in the town at special events.

# Motor Buses

Operationally more flexible than trams and trolleybus, the motor bus arrived on the scene and the major operator in Sussex was Southdown Motor Services, which spread its tendrils through most of the county and into neighbouring Hampshire, bounded by Eastbourne, Portsmouth and the Sussex border. It was formed in June 1915 from three major constituents – Worthing Motor Services, Brighton, Hove & Preston United Omnibus Co. Ltd and the London & South Coast Haulage Co. – and had various owners through its history before becoming part of the National Bus Co. in 1969. The fleet name was later lost when the company was acquired by the Stagecoach Group in 1989.

Much lamented by enthusiasts, its green-and-cream-liveried buses and coaches were a big part of their everyday lives, and it is not surprising that many Southdown vehicles are in preservation.

Eastbourne lays claim to the oldest municipally owned bus operator in the world, formed in April 1903. Running town services and longer distant services to Hailsham, Tunbridge Wells and East Grinstead, its buses wore a distinctive blue and yellow livery and bore the corporation's coat of arms. Eastbourne's long ownership ceased in 2008, when the council sold its majority shareholding in Eastbourne Buses to the Stagecoach Group.

An experimental 'tramocar' service started in Worthing in 1924, with two vehicles manufactured by Shelvoke & Drewry, a company more famous for building dustcarts. Two vehicles initially operated along the promenade, operated by Bill Gates, who sold his operations to Southdown in 1938. This example seen at Amberley is a replica body on an original S&D chassis.

Replica Southdown garage, housing ex-Southdown vehicles, and booking office at Amberley Museum & Heritage Centre.

Passengers enjoy a ride on an open-top 1920 Leyland N at Amberley Museum.

A 1930-built Southdown single-decker stops to pick up passengers at the garage at Amberley.

The 1966 Leyland Titan 'Queen Mary' on Brighton seafront.

A Southdown half-cab Leyland Titan TD3 at a bus rally.

This Brighton, Hove & District open-top Bristol K5G of 1940 has been restored by the Claude Jesset Trust at Hadlow Down.

Most traditional bus stations have been redeveloped or swept away, but a classic example still survives in Chichester. Lewes also retains its 1954 bus station.

Seen on service 2 in Churchdale Road, Eastbourne, in the late 1960s is Eastbourne Corporation's No. 35, a Crossley DD42/5 with an East Lancs Coachworks fifty-two-seat body, built in 1949. New buses were hard to come by after the war, with long order dates, so Eastbourne became the only town in the South East to have Crossleys. (David Vaughan)

The striking livery of preserved Eastbourne Corporation bus No. 42.

The first Eastbourne bus to be preserved was this 1939 Leyland Lion LT9, which remained in service until purchased for preservation in 1967. It is seen at the railway station on Eastbourne Bus Running Day 2012. (David Vaughan)

# Chapter 2

# Railways

## Standard Gauge

The independent interests that had promoted the construction of railways in Sussex soon became absorbed and operated by the London, Brighton & South Coast Railway (LB&SCR), whose territory virtually covered the county and extended to Tunbridge Wells (West) and Hastings in the east and Portsmouth and the Isle of Wight in the west. In the east, the South Eastern Railway entered Sussex on its direct route to Hastings and the London & South Western Railway entered Sussex on its route west from Petersfield to Midhurst.

## Stations

The largest and most impressive station in Sussex is Brighton, with its double-spanned iron and glass roof, fronted by a three-storey building of Italianate style designed by David Mocatta in 1839, and it is now Grade II listed. In 1971, BR Southern Region's architects Nigel Wikeley and John Middleton described the various station styles on former LB&SCR lines as 'Brighton Domestic' – with the now much-altered buildings at Buxted, Falmer and Warnham being survivors of this type, where the construction included public rooms as well as accommodation for the station master.

'Seaside' was a series of coastal stations typified by surviving examples such as Hove, London Road, Seaford and West Worthing, and the 'Hassocks type' was an 1880s series with certain mock-Tudor tendencies. The last two survivors of this type on the system at the time of the 1971 survey were at Hassocks and East Grinstead. Both were soon swiftly replaced with the then modern CLASP (Consortium of Local Authorities Special Programme) single-storey buildings of pre-fabricated frames and cladding. These did not stand the test of time and both locations have since been rebuilt to a more practical style.

The mock-Tudor stations the architects referred to as 'Hassocks type' were buildings designed by Terence H. Myers in the Norman Shaw country house style, with decorative plaster work and tile hanging, as well as stained glass top lights and entrance porch windows. Survivors include those on the Bluebell Railway at Sheffield Park, Horsted Keynes and Kingscote, and at the now-closed Ardingly station and on the 'Cuckoo Line' north of Hailsham, which can be viewed by walkers and cyclists on the Cuckoo Trail path. The surviving private dwellings at Singleton and Lavant stations on the former Chichester to Midhurst line are also of this type.

Former South Eastern Railway stations on the Tunbridge Wells to Hastings line were designed by William Tress, as was Rye station on the Hastings to Ashford line. His masterpiece is Battle station, built in the Gothic style to reflect the architecture of the nearby abbey.

The Southern Railway (1923–48) both built and rebuilt stations to their classic 1930s styles, with surviving examples at Bishopstone, Haywards Heath and Horsham.

The South Eastern Railway station at Battle has been sympathetically restored in the Gothic style.

The 1902 Grade II listed seaside terminus building at Bognor Regis.

David Mocatta's Brighton
station terminus of 1839.

Brighton's
double-spanned iron
and glass roof. Note
the hanging four-sided
LB&SCR clock.

Eastbourne's third station
building, designed for the
LB&SCR by F. D. Brick.
Note the clock tower
with the LB&SCR crest.

Hartfield station on the now-closed line from East Grinstead to Tunbridge Wells, built to the 'Brighton Domestic' style.

Horsted Keynes station as originally designed by T. H. Myers, displaying its mock Tudor plasterwork. The station is now preserved as part of the Bluebell Railway. (Bluebell Archive)

The second station at Hove, dated 1865, was restored with a grant from the Railway Heritage Trust.

*Above*: Isfield station, on the former route from Uckfield to Lewes, is now the centrepiece of the enthusiast-run Lavender Line, named after A. E. Lavender & Sons, who operated the coal yard there.

*Right*: The 'LBSC' monogram at Hove station. The ironwork of the covered porch to the west of the station entrance came second-hand from Victoria station.

The Myers-designed stations were later tile-hung in the Sussex style to protect the original plasterwork from the weather, as seen at Kingscote on the Bluebell Railway.

The present station at Lewes was the town's third, built in 1889 as a result of track remodelling, and has been tastefully restored.

The weatherboarded station at Petworth was the terminus of the Horsham to Petworth line of 1859, prior to its extension to Midhurst in 1866. Privately owned, visitors can stay overnight in the adjacent Pullman carriages or simply take afternoon tea in the restored station.

*Above*: Rye station was designed for the SER by William Tress and was built in 1851 to the Italianate style with a recessed entrance.

*Below left*: The simple but charming Rowfant station of 1855, built as the only original intermediate station on the route from Three Bridges to East Grinstead. It closed in January 1967.

*Below right*: This side porch at Rowfant provided shelter for the waiting coachman for Sir Curtis Miranda Lampson, an Anglo-American fur trader, who lived at nearby Rowfant House.

Seaford station is typical of a series of 'seaside stations' built along the Sussex coast route either side of Brighton.

Warnham station, on the Horsham to Dorking route, built to the 'Brighton Domestic' style.

The Grade II listed station at Bishopstone is a Southern Railway construction in the classic art deco style, opened in 1938. Symmetrical with an octagonal central hall and two extended wings, due to its exposed coastal position a pair of pillboxes was built on the roof, flanking the tower.

Sheffield Park station on the Bluebell Railway is an example of the T. H. Myres 'country house' style, built in 1882.

*Above and below*: Similarly styled LB&SCR platform shelters of weatherboard construction at Amberley and Warnham.

This pump house at Horsted Keynes station, on the Bluebell Railway, once housed an oil engine for pumping water from a well to service locomotives. It has been non-functional ever since a change in the water table.

## Tunnels and Viaducts

Railway tunnels penetrate the High Wealden ridge at Balcombe on the main London–Brighton line, Crowborough on the Uckfield line and Sharpthorne (now on the Bluebell Railway), but the most impressive tunnel entrance in Sussex has to be the north portal of Clayton Tunnel on the London–Brighton line, which takes the route through the South Downs. The Grade II listed portal is turreted and castellated, with a single-storey cottage at its centre, added in 1849 and designed by John Rastrick, for the purpose of housing

A Gatwick Express service for Brighton enters the north portal of Clayton Tunnel, a fine castellated and turreted structure on the main London to Brighton line that cuts through the South Downs. Note the little cottage at its centre, which is still inhabited.

Visiting new-build LNER A1 Pacific *Tornado* bursts through the northern portal of Sharpthorne Tunnel, on the Bluebell Railway, on 3 August 2014. At 731 yards long, it is the longest tunnel on a heritage railway in the UK. (Andrew Strongitharm)

a lamp-lighter who was employed to maintain gas lamps in the tunnel to allay fears of darkness by early passengers. The portal shares design details by Mocatta with his Ouse Valley Viaduct, also on the main Brighton line, and which was completed in 1841.

The Ouse Valley Viaduct is the most impressive example in Sussex. The structure is 1,480 feet long and 96 feet high with thirty-seven arches. The 11 million bricks needed for its construction came via barges up the then navigable Upper Ouse (*see Canals chapter*).

Other viaducts include London Road Viaduct in Brighton, carrying the east coastway railway line away from Brighton on a sharp curve. Built in the 1840s and designed by Rastrick, it has twenty-seven arches and is 1,200 feet long, with a wider span across Preston Road (A23), and it is Grade II listed.

Having only being used for stabling stock by British Rail following closure of the East Grinstead to Lewes line, the then disused Grade II listed Imberhorne Viaduct (formerly Hill Place Viaduct) just south of East Grinstead station now happily sees rail traffic again on the Bluebell Railway. The red brick structure is 700 feet long and 90 feet high with ten arches and was given to the Bluebell Railway's northern extension project by British Rail for a token £1.

*Above*: The Ouse Valley Viaduct near Balcombe still carries the main London to Brighton line and was completed in 1841.

*Right*: A walk beneath the Ouse Viaduct enables the tapering pier openings to be viewed.

BR Standard Class 7 No. 70013 *Oliver Cromwell* crosses the Preston Road arches of the London Road Viaduct in Brighton on 7 June 2014 with a railtour for the Seaford branch's 150th anniversary celebrations.

LB&SCR E4 No. B473 takes a train of vintage L&SWR and SR stock over the red brick Imberhorne Viaduct, on the Bluebell Railway, on 6 March 2016. (Andrew Strongitharm)

# Signal Boxes

It wasn't so long ago that mechanically-operated signal boxes were part of the everyday railway scene, housing the signalman and the equipment that controlled the signals and points. Advances in technology have seen the rapid decline of these structures and much of the Sussex routes are now controlled from a modern operating centre at Three Bridges on the main London–Brighton line.

Many signal boxes in Sussex have either been demolished or have been removed and rebuilt elsewhere, while some redundant examples have become listed structures in their own right. Listed Sussex boxes include those at Berwick; Billingshurst (moved to Amberley Museum in 2014); Chichester; Eastbourne; Horsham; Horsted Keynes (Bluebell Railway); Isfield (Lavender Line); Littlehampton; Plumpton; Pulborough; and Rye. Any redundant boxes that were not listed were demolished with indecent haste by Network Rail.

Traditional signal boxes still 'manned' at the time of publication (although some are switch panel operated rather than mechanical) are at Arundel; Bognor Regis; Bo-Peep Junction; Chichester; Hastings; Lancing; Lewes; Littlehampton; Newhaven Harbour; Newhaven Town; Robertsbridge; and Rye. Barnham box, a later structure housing a modern switch panel, replaced a traditional box that was moved to a site adjacent to Bognor Regis Model Railway Club at Aldingbourne. The top portion of the former Uckfield Shunting Cabin box now functions as a bird hide on the railway land nature reserve at Lewes. The former box at Withyham (closed 1967) is now part of the Bluebell Railway's museum at Sheffield Park, where visitors can operate a signal in the traditional manner.

The listed Saxby & Farmer Type 5 signal box at Berwick, erected in 1879 and now disused.

*Above*: The Grade II listed Billingshurst signal box represents Saxby & Farmer's initial 1b design, a development of the Saxby 1a, and is believed to have been at an earlier location prior to erection at Billingshurst in 1876. Surplus to requirements by 2014, it was moved to Amberley Museum and was re-erected, opening next to the narrow gauge line in March 2018.

*Left*: The Grade II listed Saxby & Farmer 1877 signal box at Crawley once controlled a level crossing bottleneck on the main London to Brighton road before the advent of the Crawley Bypass. It was made redundant in 1978 and is now in the care of a local preservation society and is open to visitors once a month.

The now disused and listed Saxby & Farmer Type 5 box at Eastbourne was built in 1882, originally housing an impressive 108-lever frame.

Hastings signal box represents the first universal design to be built by the Southern Railway, being erected in 1930 to replace three traditional boxes in the area. It still controls traditional semaphore signalling but surely its days are now numbered.

This Southern Railway art deco style Type 13 signal box at Horsham closed in 2005 but is now Grade II listed as an example of the larger two-storey type, with the operating floor above and equipment and staff accommodation below.

Still controlling traditional semaphore signalling is the 1886 Type 2 box, seen on the right of the photograph, at Littlehampton. It is now Grade II listed and its survival, past the onset of modernisation, is assured.

Surely now on borrowed time are the signal boxes at Newhaven Town and Newhaven Harbour, controlling the branch line between Newhaven and the terminus at Seaford. Newhaven Town signal box is a Saxby & Farmer Type 5 of *c.* 1879 and, amazingly, its two surviving locking room windows are still glazed.

*Right*: Plumpton signal box was opened in 1891 and the box and its traditional crossing gates were Grade II listed. Famed for being the last wheel-worked crossing gates in Sussex, closure came in 2015 when Network Rail replaced the listed gates with barriers controlled from Three Bridges in a closure stand-off with the local council that was trying to protect them.

*Below*: The disused Grade II listed Pulborough signal box is a Saxby & Farmer Type 5 example, built in 1878, and is the only example of a two-bay, six-window-width Type 5 in the country.

Uckfield signal box of 1858, which once controlled crossing gates on the busy A22 London–Eastbourne road before the town was bypassed, now functions as a taxi control office.

# Goods Sheds

Purpose-built goods sheds were once a common sight on our railways, but from the late 1950s to early 1960s, when road transport improved so that goods could be taken from door to door, their days were numbered. Commuters' car parks and retail or housing developments have swallowed disused goods sidings and their sheds along with them, although there are still some remarkable twenty-first-century survivors.

The two-storey brick goods shed at Arundel is a particularly fine survivor from the days of transporting goods by rail.

Hartfield goods shed has undergone a sympathetic restoration to become the local parish council offices.

The goods shed at the former junction station of Pulborough is now an auto repair centre.

A typical LB&SCR country station timber-built goods 'lock-up', preserved at Kingscote, on the Bluebell Railway. It was formerly at Horsted Keynes, two stations to the south.

# Level Crossings

The level crossing gates at Bodiam (and Northiam) on the preserved Kent & East Sussex Railway are the last standard gauge level crossing gates in Sussex to be worked by hand.

Built by the Brighton & Chichester Railway, this brick and flint 1840s crossing keeper's cottage survives at Ferring, near Worthing.

Although non-operational, this fine set of level crossing gates remain in situ at Isfield on the former Uckfield to Lewes line.

The crossing keeper's cottage at Plumpton.

# Other Standard Gauge Railways

The West Sussex Railway (Hundred of Manhood & Selsey Tramway) opened in 1897 from Chichester to Selsey and was built as a light railway with its construction supervised by engineer Holman F. Stephens. It enjoyed some success before the First World War but suffered when road transport increased in the 1920s. Steam was replaced with petrol-driven railcars in an efficiency drive but these could not halt the inevitable decline and the route closed to all traffic in 1935.

With the formation mostly at ground level, there is very little trace of the line to be found today. However, there is a section that is now a public footpath west of Hunston, as well as a farm track between Pagham Harbour and Selsey Golf Club.

The Hellingly Hospital Railway was another line built to light railway standards and was constructed in 1899 to serve the psychiatric hospital at Hellingly via a 1.25-mile-long line from the LB&SCR's Hellingly station on the Eridge to Polegate 'Cuckoo Line'. Passengers transferring from main line trains to hospital trains used a small wooden platform opposite the station and the line was also used for transporting goods, such as provisions and coal for the hospital's furnaces. The East Sussex County Council-owned line was electrified in 1903 at 500 V DC by way of a single overhead line via a trolley pole. Passenger transportation on the line had ceased by 1931 and the conversion of the hospital boilers from coal to oil ended the need for a railway, albeit one that never had a timetable, and the line officially closed on 25 March 1959. Little of the route remains and the site of the demolished hospital has now been given over to housing.

These concrete bridge abutments carried the West Sussex Railway across the Chichester Canal, near Hunston.

An enamel sign promoting the Selsey Tramway, displayed at the Colonel Stephens Museum, Tenterden.

Drawing power from the single overhead line, the electric locomotive and single coal wagon reverses from Hellingly station sidings, prior to turning on to the branch for the hospital (right).

The route of the Hellingly Hospital Railway at Park Road crossing. The gate is possibly original and would have been opened by the tramway driver.

The last remaining trolley pole from this system is in the garden of 'The Lodge', Park Road – visible from the field alongside.

# Narrow Gauge

Pride of place for the first 'railway' in Sussex goes to the tramway line that linked a chalk quarry with barges on the River Ouse at Offham, near Lewes. The stone block 'sleepers' used in its construction came from a quarry at Wych Cross and were transported by oxen to Sheffield Bridge, and from there by river barge to Offham. It opened in 1825 and survived until 1870.

Narrow gauge railways, for public transportation and for industry requirements, were to be found around the county. Built to serve industrial sites, they included the internal systems at the brickworks at Berwick, Bexhill, Crowborough, and Warnham and Pepper's lime works at Amberley. Extractive industries made use of lines at Rodmell Cement Works, Cuckmere Haven, Eartham and Heavers of Chichester (gravel). Chichester Sewage Works had its own railway, as did Mountfield Gypsum Works.

Although intended for goods rather than passengers, it is still possible in the twenty-first century to find out how this type of railway operated – and take a ride – thanks to the narrow gauge lines at Amberley Museum & Heritage Centre and the Great Bush Railway at Hadlow Down. Both railways have examples of motive power and wagons that previously ran on long-closed Sussex systems.

The most well-known narrow gauge line from a public perspective is Volk's Electric Railway on Brighton seafront. Magnus Volk, the son of a German immigrant clockmaker, who had already experimented with electricity in the form of establishing the first telephone link in Brighton and fitting his own house with electric lighting, opened the first public electric railway in Britain on 4 August 1883. A car for twelve passengers ran for about 300 yards at 6 mph along a 2 foot gauge track, then extended to 1,400 yards the next season at 2 foot 9 inch gauge before finally settling on 2 foot 8.5 inch gauge.

The entrance to the twin tunnels that carried the Offham Tramway can still be viewed, adjacent to the car park of the former Chalk Pit Inn. Originally the quarry offices, it is now an Indian restaurant.

Initially running between Aquarium and the Chain Pier it has been both extended and reduced in length over the years for several reasons. Now operating from Aquarium to Black Rock (Brighton Marina), the railway is maintained and operated by Brighton & Hove City Council and was a recipient of a Heritage Lottery Fund grant of £1.65 million in 2015, which saw the attraction re-open in early 2018 with upgraded track, cars and a car shed depot, as well as a new Aquarium station that now incorporates a visitor centre.

Supplied new in 1899, this Aveling & Porter locomotive was one of two at Pepper & Sons' lime works at Amberley until replaced with a new diesel loco in 1953. (J. H. Mere)

Seen at Glyne Gap Gasworks near Bexhill, this 1896 Bagnall 0-4-0ST was purchased second-hand in 1926. (J. H. Meredith)

Seen on 26 September 1952, this 100 hp Sentinel shunter was new to Mountfield Gypsum Mine in 1948 and lasted there until 1967. (J. B. Latham)

Ruston Hornsby No. 5 *Alpha* was recovered from the Associated Portland Cement Works at Rodmell and is now at the Great Bush Railway.

Wingrove & Rogers No. M7535 of 1972 (No. 24 *Titch*) was new to Crowborough Brickworks, and is now at the Great Bush Railway.

Wingrove & Rogers
No. 5033 of 1953
(No. 22 *Lama*)
was transferred
to Crowborough
Brickworks from
Dorking in 1972, and is
now at the Great Bush
Railway.

The Great Bush
Railway's Motor Rail
No. 8687 of 1941
(No. 4 *Mild*) transferred
to Crowborough in 1971
from Hampshire.

This 1941 Hudson
Hunslet locomotive,
previously located at
Thakeham Tile Works
near Storrington, is now
preserved at Amberley
Museum.

*Right*: Robert Hudson of Leeds petrol/ paraffin (Fordson) tractor No. 4591 of 1932 worked at Midhurst Whites Ltd brickworks at Midhurst and is now at Amberley Museum.

*Below*: A Robert Hudson skip wagon chassis, now used for permanent way duties on the Great Bush Railway.

*Above left*: Built in Berlin, Orenstein & Koppel No. 11784 *Sao Domingos* of 1928 worked in Portugal all of its life and was imported into the UK in 1972. It is seen coming off shed at the Great Bush Railway. (Alan Barnes)

*Above right*: Narrow gauge travel can be experienced on the Great Bush Railway.

*Below*: A Hunslet locomotive hauls a passenger train on the narrow gauge railway at Amberley Museum.

Hawthorn Leslie 0-4-0ST No. 2532 of 1902 (*No. 17 Atlas*) was new to Atlas Steel Works, Sheffield, and moved to Eastwoods Cement Co., Lewes, in 1932. The Avonside worksplates seen here belonged to *Anne* and *Mary*, two locos from Sydenham Gas Works that moved to Eastbourne Gas Works *c*. 1960.

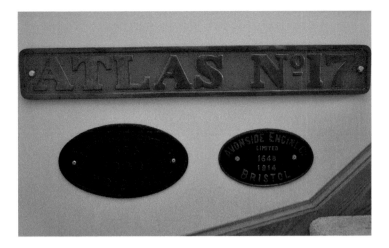

Volk's Railway at Brighton – Britain's first public electric railway, and still operating.

The new Aquarium station at Volk's Railway, incorporating an upgraded ticket office and visitor centre.

Volk started work in 1894 on the Brighton & Rottingdean Seashore Electric Tramroad, which ran for a distance of nearly 3 miles. The track had an overall gauge of 18 feet and was laid on concrete blocks built into the foreshore some 60 yards from the cliff face. The passenger car was supported on four 24-foot-long legs, carrying the drive and brake shafts to the wheels, running on rails and taking power from an overhead wire. Soon dubbed the 'Daddy Longlegs' on account of its appearance, as it was effectively 'at sea' the Board of Trade insisted that a lifeboat be provided. Speed was limited to 8 mph and a telephone was fitted for emergency use. The concrete 'sleeper' blocks that carried the track can be viewed east of the Marina at low tide.

The Sea Car.        Brighton.

*Above*: Volk's 'sea car' of the Brighton & Rottingdean Seashore Electric Tramroad, which was dubbed the 'Daddy Longlegs'.

*Left*: The concrete 'sleepers' that carried the tracks of the 'Daddy Longlegs' can be observed along the foreshore at low tide. (Carol Homewood)

74

# The Rye & Camber Tramway

Initially built in 1895 to carry golfers from Rye station to their golf club, the 3 foot gauge line, designed by Holman F. Stephens, was extended to Camber Sands in 1908. Operated by Bagnall locomotives and a Motor Rail type petrol engine, the line did not recover from its worn out state following the Second World War.

*Above*: Camber station on the Rye & Camber Tramway, 1931.

*Right*: A surviving lantern from Rye, on display at the Colonel Stephens Museum, Tenterden.

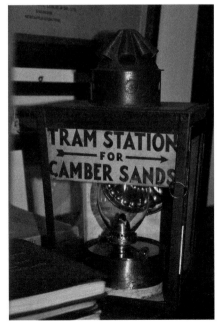

# Cliff Lifts

There are two cliff lifts in Sussex – Hastings East and West Hill lifts. The East Hill lift – opened in 1903, and now the UK's steepest surviving funicular railway at a gradient of 78 per cent – is of 5 foot gauge and is 267 feet in length. It was originally worked via the water balance principle, with each car carrying a water tank that was filled at the upper station and emptied at the lower. Electrification came in the mid-1970s. The lower station is accessed from Rock-a-Nore by the old fisherman's huts on the Stade and provides transport to Hastings Country Park.

The West Hill lift is of earlier construction, being built in 1890, and, running largely through a tunnel at a gradient of 33 per cent, is of 6 foot gauge and is 500 feet in length. Originally powered by a gas engine and then an oil engine, it is now electrically operated. The lower station is on George Street and the lift gives access to St Clement's Caves and Hastings Castle.

Both lifts are now maintained and operated by Hastings Borough Council and are open from 10 a.m. to 5.30 p.m. in season.

The Hastings East Hill lift of 1903 is now the steepest surviving funicular railway in the UK.

The Hastings West Hill lift of 1890 is mostly in tunnel.

# Heritage Railways

The Bluebell Railway, which runs 11 miles from Sheffield Park to East Grinstead on the route of the former Lewes & East Grinstead line, can claim its place in British history as the first standard gauge (full size) former British Railways line to be run by volunteers, opening in August 1960. Its members had seen the success of 1950s narrow gauge preservation in Wales and felt that they could make a good job of 'upscaling' a line that had received much national publicity following an 'illegal' closure in 1955 by BR, resulting in re-opening and a second, final, closure in 1958. The tourist heritage line, with its thirty-three steam locomotives, eighty-nine carriages and eighty-three wagons, remains a benchmark for the many preserved railways that were to start up around Britain, now a multi-million pound industry.

Holman F. Stephens (later Colonel) was also responsible for the Rother Valley Railway, which left the main Tunbridge Wells to Hastings line at Robertsbridge and ran to Tenterden, Kent, becoming the Kent & East Sussex Railway on its extension from Tenterden to Headcorn (the latter becoming the name for the whole line). Revivalists re-opened the stretch from Tenterden to Rolvended in Kent before extending westwards to Wittersham Road (1977), entering Sussex and then going on to Northiam (1990) and Bodiam (2000). Built to light railway standards, the operators have maintained the utilitarian heritage of its stations and atmosphere.

A separate company, Rother Valley Railway, has been formed to replace the missing link from Robertsbridge, eastwards to Bodiam, to again link the two sections. Much work has been undertaken at Robertsbridge while awaiting statutory permissions to rebuild the line.

The Lavender Line is a 1-mile stretch of re-opened railway, based at Isfield on the former Uckfield to Lewes route, which was closed by BR in 1969. Revival came in 1983 when the Isfield site was purchased by landscaper Dave Milham, who set up home in the station house and operated a limited train service on the restored site. Mr Milham passed ownership to the preservation society in 1991, which has continued to operate steam, diesel and DMU services in season.

Sheffield Park station on the Bluebell Railway is restored to how it would have appeared in the Victorian period of the LB&SCR.

The Bluebell Railway's first locomotive was LB&SCR A1X Terrier *Stepney*, a children's favourite that featured in the *Thomas the Tank Engine* series. (Martin Lawrence)

The strong Southern Railway atmosphere recreated at the Bluebell Railway, with SR S15 Class No. 847 and Southern coaching stock. (Andrew Strongitharm)

SR Q Class No. 30541 passes the Grade II listed Horsted Keynes South signal box with a goods train on the Bluebell Railway. (Andrew Strongitharm)

Bodiam station on the Kent & East Sussex Railway is typical of Colonel Stephen's light railways utilitarian style.

USA Class tank No. DS238, as Longmoor Military Railway No. 300 waits for the gates to open before departing from Bodiam to return to Tenterden.

BR P Class No. 31556 *Pride of Sussex*, seen on 30 September 1961, when in the ownership of Hodson's Mill at Robertsbridge. (D. W. Winkworth)

The new Robertsbridge Junction station, on the Rother Valley Railway, will eventually become the eastern terminus of the Kent & East Sussex Railway.

The Lavender Line's Thumper DEMU No. 1133, built in 1962, is seen at Eridge in 2015 while visiting the Spa Valley Railway.

The Spa Valley Railway is a heritage steam and diesel operation running on the former Eridge to Tunbridge Wells line, which was closed by BR in 1985. It is another line that is based in Kent, but extends into Sussex. It shares the station at Eridge with Network Rail's route to Uckfield from Oxted, returning the station once again to 'country junction' status. The line is noted for having saved one of the former much-loved DEMU Thumper units that ran on this line until closure – the type initially built to act as a stop gap between steam and eventual electrification on East Sussex lines. Only the lines to Hastings and East Grinstead were eventually electrified, and the sections from Hurst Green to Uckfield and Hastings to Rye remain DMU-worked to this day.

*Above*: Preserved DEMU No. 1137 is based at the Spa Valley Railway and recreates a once typical Sussex secondary line scene, of a type that ultimately lasted for forty-seven years in service.

*Left*: Preservation group Hastings Diesels Ltd maintain examples of the iconic former Charing Cross–Hastings line narrow-bodied DEMUs to main line standard and undertake frequent railtours across the Southern network and beyond.

# Chapter 3

# Carriage by Water

## Ports

The importance of the sea to Sussex has been crucial through its history and its proximity to the continent has brought forth invaders of all sorts over thousands of years, including the most important and famous invasion of 1066. Harbours brought goods such as building materials and foodstuffs, and provided employment to boat builders and sailors. Shoreham is the only Sussex port mentioned in a seventeenth-century survey of shipbuilding. Fishing boats could be found on beaches throughout the county and fishing smacks of Sussex oak were built on the river banks at Rye Strand until the beginning of the twentieth century.

Important medieval harbours once included Chichester, Shoreham, Seaford, Rye and Winchelsea. Pevensey was already silting up by then and most of the others followed.

NEWHAVEN, SUSSEX." SWING BRIDGE CARRYING PUBLIC ROAD OVER THE HARBOUR.    *Waterlow & Sons Ltd.*

The original swing bridge across the Ouse at Newhaven, now replaced with a modern version. Ironwork and lanterns from the original bridge can be viewed at Newhaven Museum, situated at the town's Paradise Park.

Chichester had finished as a commercial port by the end of the Second World War but trade had already dropped steadily following the arrival of the Brighton to Portsmouth railway. The harbour area is now given over to leisure craft.

The catalyst for the decline of Littlehampton as a port came with the decision by the London, Brighton & South Coast Railway to withdraw cross-Channel steamers in 1882, favouring the newly cut harbour at Meeching (the 'new haven'), which it owned. This was compounded by the decline in the need for wooden sailing vessels built at Littlehampton's main shipyard.

Newhaven remains the port for the Dieppe ferry route, while Shoreham retains its position as the county's busiest commercial port. It remains the nearest channel port to London and was at the height of its importance in the twelfth and thirteenth centuries.

The mouth of the River Ouse at Newhaven.

The only remaining cross-Channel ferry from Sussex is the (French-owned) Newhaven to Dieppe service, which runs twice daily and three times in summer. The ferry *Seven Sisters* waits at Newhaven.

The mouth of the River Arun at Littlehampton, once an important port for goods and early cross-Channel packet boats.

The dredger *Sand Heron* awaits permission to leave the port of Shoreham.

# Inland Waterways

Sussex may not have had the great swathes of inland waterways of the scale that connected the large industrial towns and ports of the north of England, but the short heyday of the cuts and navigations in Sussex brought a means of carrying coal, aggregates for road improvements, manure, chalk and lime as an improvement in transportation when compared with the poor condition of the roads. The canals were in turn superseded by the arrival of the railways.

# Adur Navigation (Baybridge)

A short stretch of 3.5-mile-long canal was opened in 1826 (and abandoned by 1875) with the aim of improving access for boats from next to the Horsham to Worthing Turnpike (now A24) to Bines Bridge on the River Adur, which can be seen beside the B2135 near Partridge Green.

# The Portsmouth & Arundel Canal

Built in 1823 by the Portsmouth & Arundel Navigation Company, and ceasing operation in 1855, the canal consisted of three sections with the aim of securing an inland route for traffic between the towns without heading into the Channel. Little remains of the Ford to Hunston section. Birdham Lock is visible on the Birdham to Hunston section (SU 826012). The Chichester Canal from Birdham to Chichester is navigable and was once part of the P&A Canal.

The Chichester Ship Canal at Hunston.

Day-trippers board the narrow boat *Richmond* for a tour of the Chichester canals.

# The Rother Navigation

Construction started in 1791 and opened in 1793 to link Petworth and Midhurst with the sea via the River Arun. Engineer William Jessop surveyed the River Rother for the 3rd Earl of Egremont, with 2 miles of cuts on an improved and widened 12-mile navigation with eight locks. The heyday of goods barges on the route was from 1823 until 1859, and it was abandoned in 1888 (TQ 033182 to SU 887213.)

The remains of Coultershaw bridge and lock on the Rother Navigation, which opened in 1793 and closed in 1888.

# The Upper Ouse Navigation

The tidal Sussex Ouse, south of Lewes and down to Newhaven, had long been used by commercial vessels, but William Jessop was appointed to survey the Upper Ouse north of Lewes in 1787 with a view to extending navigation, initially to Slaugham, but this was never reached. The Upper Ouse Navigation Act was passed and construction commenced, with completion to Upper Rylands Bridge in 1812, near the Ouse Valley Viaduct on the London–Brighton railway line. Indeed, the 11 million bricks used to construct the viaduct in 1841 were transported via the navigation. The 22-mile route featured nineteen locks and a ¾-mile spur to Shortbridge via a wharf at Maresfield. Commercial activity north of Lewes had ceased by the 1860s but the tidal stretch south of the town saw boats until the 1950s. Most of the locks are still extant, although are slowly deteriorating. Volunteers of the Sussex Ouse Restoration Trust work to conserve the structures of the navigation.

*Above*: One of the most complete lock chambers to survive on the Upper Ouse Navigation is at Bacon Wish, one lock up-river from Sheffield Bridge on the A275. It opened in 1798 and closed in 1868. (Phil Barnes)

*Left*: The last surviving farmers' occupation bridge over the Upper Ouse at Bacon Wish Lock. (Phil Barnes)

When commercial traffic on the Upper Ouse arrived, so did public houses to serve the needs of bargemen, including the Sloop Inn at Freshfield (pictured) and The Anchor at Barcombe.

The navigable Ouse reached just beyond Upper Ryelands Bridge, where these wharf cottages survive on Borde Hill Lane.

# Royal Military Canal

Constructed in 1806 by consulting engineer John Rennie as a coastal defence against possible invasion during the Napoleonic Wars, the 28-mile canal runs from Hythe in Kent and into Sussex, ending at Iden Lock (TQ 936244). A second, smaller section runs wholly in Sussex from Winchelsea (TQ 908175) to Cliff End (TQ 886129).

# Wey & Arun Junction Canal

From Shalford on the River Wey in Surrey (and on to the River Thames) down to Pallingham Lock at the River Arun (and on to the sea at Littlehampton), 23 miles of canal with twenty-six locks were opened in 1816, engineered by William Jessop's son, Josias. The canal lasted commercially for just over fifty years, providing an efficient route from London to Portsmouth to carry goods supplying the dockyards.

The Wey & Arun Canal Trust was formed in 1970 to restore 'London's Lost Route to the Sea' as an extremely long-term project. Volunteers have so far restored twenty-four bridges and eleven locks. The Trust's information and visitor centre is located adjacent to the Onslow Arms on the navigation at Loxwood (TQ 41311) and the Trust's boats give the public trips from the adjacent jetty south to Drungewick and north to Brewhurst. The explorer of today can view the only canal tunnel in Sussex (TQ 033171) and the only aqueduct in Sussex (at TQ 058246), both on disused stretches of canal.

The restored bridge and lock at Loxwood on the Wey & Arun Canal.

The Wey & Arun Canal Trust's narrow boat *Zachariah Keppel* heads south from Loxwood with a tour party.

Lordings Aqueduct, the only aqueduct in Sussex, is a three-arch structure taking the Wey & Arun Canal across the River Arun. Now restored by volunteers, it is on a section of canal yet to be re-opened. (Wey & Arun Canal Trust Ltd)

The south portal of the only canal tunnel in Sussex at Hardham, built as part of a cut to avoid a 3-mile meander in the Arun. The last barge passed through here on 29 January 1889. Passing under the LB&SCR's Mid-Sussex line and its line from Pulborough to Petworth, the railway dug down and blocked the tunnel to 'stabilise its lines' in 1898.

# Chapter 4

# Airports

## Gatwick Airport

Gatwick, London's 'second airport' after Heathrow, and the busiest single runway airport until 2017 (now Mumbai), had much more humble beginnings.

The descendants of the de Gatwick family sold the area to the Gatwick Race Course Company in 1890, the racecourse being adjacent to a dedicated station on the London to Brighton main line. The course was the venue of the Grand National from 1916 to 1918 and closed at the start of the Second World War when the adjacent aerodrome, opened in the late 1290s, was requisitioned by the military.

Originally in Surrey but located in West Sussex since the local authority boundary changes of 1974, Gatwick Airport has been used for commercial flights since 1933 (TQ 285401). The previous aerodrome terminal, based in a converted farmhouse, was closed in 1935 to allow a new terminal to be built. Completed in early 1936, the new

Early days at Gatwick. A British Airways Dutch-built Fokker FXII prepares to depart on the new service for Le Bourget in May 1935, carrying sixteen passengers and a crew of two. Note the 'Beehive' terminal behind. (Iris Publishing/Hulton)

Gatwick's 1936 art deco terminal building survives as offices, although planes no longer come up alongside.

terminal was constructed in reinforced concrete in the art deco style of the period to create a modern impression. Recognised as having been the UK's first integrated airport building, combining all necessary facilities under one roof, its single storey rises to three at its centre, with the central section containing a control tower. Affectionately named 'The Beehive', it too was adjacent to a station on the Brighton main line, effectively becoming the UK's first 'rail-air link' facility. The government announced in 1952 that Gatwick would be London's 'second' airport and more land was acquired, including the old racecourse. The main London–Brighton A23 road was diverted around the airport boundary and a new terminal was constructed by 1958. The 1935-built Gatwick Airport station closed and a new airport station was built to the north, on the site of the previous racecourse station. After many improvements through the decades, this new terminal is now the South Terminal, and a new North Terminal was constructed in the 1980s. The airport handled 46 million passengers in 2017.

# Shoreham Airport

Officially known as Brighton City Airport, Shoreham is the second oldest airport in the UK, being founded in 1910, with the aerodrome opening in June 1911. A new terminal building in the art deco style of the period was designed by Stavers Tiltman and was built in 1936 under the umbrella of the 'Brighton Hove and Worthing Joint Municipal Airport', with the building receiving Grade II listing in 1984.

The LB&SCR opened Bungalow Town Halt, on its coastal line from Brighton to Chichester, in the vicinity of the airport in 1910. It was renamed Shoreham Airport in 1935 and was closed in 1940.

Traffic at the airport is now primarily drawn from private light aircraft, flying schools, helicopter maintenance and pleasure flights. The airport's pre-war hangar was listed as Grade II in 2007.

The 1936-built terminal of the Brighton Hove and Worthing Joint Municipal Airport at Shoreham.

Facade detail at Shoreham Airport – much requested for a role in period films.

# Museums

Where to see examples of our glorious transport heritage:

**Amberley Museum & Heritage Centre**
Amberley, near Arundel, BN18 9LT (www.amberleymuseum.co.uk)

**Bentley Motor Museum**
Ringmer, Lewes, BN8 5AF (www.bentley.org.uk)

**Bluebell Railway**
Sheffield Park, near Uckfield, TN22 3QL (www.bluebell-railway.com)

**Chichester Canal Visitor Centre**
Canal Wharf, Chichester, PO19 8DT (www.chichestercanal.org.uk)

**Gatwick Aviation Museum**
Charlwood, RH6 0BT (www.gatwick-aviation-museum.co.uk)

**Lavender Line**
Isfield, TN22 5XB (www.lavender-line.co.uk)

**Spa Valley Railway**
Eridge Station, TN3 9LE (www.spavalleyrailway.co.uk)

**Volks Electric Railway**
Brighton, BN2 1EN (www.volksrailway.org.uk)

**Wey & Arun Canal**
Loxwood, RH14 0RH (www.weyarun.org.uk)

# Bibliography

Austen, B., Cox, D. and Upton, J., *Sussex Industrial Archaeology: A Field Guide* (Chichester: Phillimore & Co. Ltd, 1985).

Harley, R. J., *Brighton's Tramways* (Midhurst: Middleton Press, 1992).

Hart, B., *The Kent & East Sussex Railway* (Didcot: Wild Swan Publications).

Hill, A. F., *Lower Ouse Navigation* (Lewes: 1991).

Mitchell, V. and Smith, K., *Sussex Narrow Gauge* (Midhurst: Middleton Press, 2001).

Oppitz, L., *Sussex Railways Remembered* (Newbury: Countryside Books, 1987).

Various, *Industrial Railways of the South East* (Midhurst: Middleton Press, 1984).

Wikeley, N. and Middleton, J., *Railway Stations Southern Region* (Seaton: Peco Publications, 1971).

www.wikipedia.org.